The vibrant Keto Diet Recipe Collection

Discover the perfect diet to feel great in your 50s

Samantha Bennett

TABLE OF CONTENTS

BREAKFAST **8**

Coco-Coffee Mug 9

Breakfast Pudding 10

Green Breakfast Smoothie..................................... 11

Chocolate Granola 13

Raw Muesli 14

Scrambled Tofu...15

BRUNCH **17**

Coleslaw with Eggs 18

Traditional Spinach and Feta Frittata.................... 20

Italian-style Keto Sandwiches 22

Spinach and Eggs Salad... 24

Curried Deviled Eggs 26

SOUP AND STEWS **27**

Red Gazpacho 28

Tomato & Basil Soup 30

Salsa Verde Chicken Soup 32

Broccoli Soup... 34

Cauliflower Soup with Kielbasa 36

Bacon Stew with Cauliflower.................................37

MAIN **38**

Zucchini Noodle Carbonara 39

Radish & Zucchini Quiche 41

Quattro Formaggi Pizza 43

Keto Soufflé with Chorizo Sausage 45

Vodka Cauliflower Casserole 47

MEAT **49**

Pork with Olives 50

Szechuan Beef Stir Fry 51

Savory Pork Tacos 53

Roasted Spicy Beef 56

Delicious Sausage Salad 58

Beef Shanks Braised in Red Wine Sauce 59

Herbed Grilled Lamb 61

Coconut and Lime Steak 63

POULTRY **65**

Almond Crusted Chicken Zucchini Stacks 66

So Delicious Chicken Wings 67

Chicken and Mushrooms 69

Creamy Chicken Thighs with Capers 71

FISH **73**

Pistachio-crusted Salmon 74

Cod Fillets with Tangy Sesame Sauce 76

Fried Salmon with Asparagus 77

Shrimp Wraps 79

Catfish & Cauliflower Casserole 81

Trout and Endives 83

Scallops with Broccoli... 84

VEGETABLES **86**

Classic Tangy Ratatouille 87

Garlicky Bok Choy 89

Cheesy Zucchini Bake..91

Mixed Veggie Salad 93

Broccoli Slaw Salad with Mustard-mayo Dressing.................95

DESSERT.. **96**

Simple Chocolate Tart 97

Chocolate Chip Blondies 100

Strawberry Stew...103

Passion Fruit Cheesecake Slices 104

Lemon Mug Cake...106

Strawberry Mousse..107

content within this book has been derived from various sources. Please consult a licensed professional before attempting any techniques outlined in this book. By reading this document, the reader agrees that under no circumstances is the author responsible for any losses, 5 direct or indirect, which are incurred as a result of the use of information contained within this document, including, but not limited to, — errors, omissions, or inaccuracies.

BREAKFAST

Coco-Coffee Mug

Servings: 1

Preparation Time: 5 minutes

Ingredients:

- Flaxseed -ground: 2 tablespoon
- Coconut flakes -unsweetened: 2 tablespoon
- Coconut oil: 1 tablespoon
- Liquid sweetener: to taste
- Black coffee -unsweetened: ½ cup

Directions:

1. Mix together the coconut flakes, coconut oil, and flaxseed.

2. Pour the hot coffee over it and mix well along with the sweetener.

Nutrition Value:

277 Cal, 27 g total fat, 7g carb., 5 g fiber, 4 g protein.

Breakfast Pudding

Servings: 3

Preparation Time: 5 minutes

Ingredients:

- Coconut milk -full-fat: 1 ½ cup
- Frozen raspberries: 1 cup
- MCT oil: ¼ cup
- Apple cider vinegar: 1 tablespoon
- Vanilla extract: 1 teaspoon
- Stevia: 3 drops
- Chia seeds: 2 tablespoons
- Fresh berries: for topping

Directions:

1. Combine all the ingredients in a food processor.
2. Blend until smooth.
3. Serve chilled topped with fresh berries.

Nutrition Value:

328 Cal, 34.2 g total fat -30.8 g sat. fat, 8.8g carb., 3.1 g fiber, 3.2 g protein.

Green Breakfast Smoothie

Servings: 1

Preparation Time: 5 minutes

Ingredients:

- Almond milk: 1 ½ cup
- Spinach: 1 oz.
- Cucumber: 1 ¾ oz.
- Celery: 1 ¾ oz.
- Avocado: 1 ¾ oz.
- Coconut oil: 1 tablespoon
- Liquid stevia: 10 drops
- Isopure Protein powder: 1 scoop
- Chia seeds: ½ teaspoon

Directions:

1. Blend together the spinach and almond milk in a blender.
2. Mix in the rest of the ingredients except the chia seeds and blend until smooth and creamy.
3. Serve garnished with chia seeds.

Nutrition Value:

375 Cal, 25 g total fat, 4 g net carb., 30 g protein.

Chocolate Granola

Servings: 32

Preparation Time: 10 minutes

Cooking Time: 20 minutes

Ingredients:

- Sunflower seeds: 3.5 oz.
- Almonds -chopped: 3.5 oz.
- Walnuts -chopped: 3.5 oz.
- Flax seeds: 3.5 oz.

Directions:

1. Mix together the coconut oil, cinnamon, sweetener, and cocoa powder.
2. Toss together all the nuts, seeds, and coconut in a baking dish and pour the cocoa mixture over, stirring well.
3. Bake for 20 minutes at 350 degrees Fahrenheit until crisp and brown, tossing every 4 minutes.

Nutrition Value:

187 Cal, 17.5 g total fat, 6.2 g carb., 4 g fibre, 4.3 g protein.

Raw Muesli

Servings: 20

Preparation Time: 5 minutes

Ingredients:

- Shredded Coconut -unsweetened: 2 cups
- Pumpkin seeds: 1 cup
- Walnut pieces: 1 cup
- Almonds -chopped: 1 cup
- Sunflower seeds: 1 cup
- Sesame seeds: 1 cup
- Linseed -ground: 1 cup

Directions:

1. Combine all the ingredients together and seal in an airtight jar.
2. Serve with coconut cream.

Nutrition Value:

298 Cal, 26 g total fat, 8.6 g carb., 4.4 g fibre, 9.4 g protein.

Scrambled Tofu

Servings: 2

Preparation Time: 10 minutes

Cooking Time: 20 minutes

Ingredients:

- Extra-firm tofu -pat dried: 8 oz.
- Red onion -sliced thinly: ¼
- Kale -chopped: 2 cups
- Olive oil: 2 tablespoon
- Sea salt: ½ teaspoon
- Chili powder: ¼ teaspoon
- Garlic powder: ½ teaspoon
- Turmeric: ¼ teaspoon
- Cumin powder: ½ teaspoon

Directions:

1. Mix together the dry spices, salt, and some water in a bowl to make the sauce.
2. Heat oil in a skillet and sauté the red pepper and onion in it, seasoning with a pinch of salt and pepper.
3. Mix in the kale and steam covered for 2 minutes.
4. Crumble the tofu into small pieces and add the tofu to the skillet, sautéing for 2 minutes.
5. Pour in the sauce and stir well.
6. Cook for 5-7 minutes.

Nutrition Value:

252 Cal, 19 g total fat -3 g sat. fat, 516 mg sodium, 12.7 g carb., 3 g fibre, 12 g protein.

BRUNCH

Coleslaw with Eggs

Servings: 4

Cooking Time: 15 minutes

Ingredients

- 3 cups cabbage, shredded
- 2 large eggs, boiled
- 1 ½ tablespoon Dijon Mustard
- ½ cup mayonnaise
- ½ teaspoon salt
- ½ teaspoon pepper
- 2 tablespoons fresh parsley, chopped
- 1 teaspoon poppy seeds
- 1 tablespoon white vinegar

Directions:

1. In a small bowl, prepare the dressing by mixing the Dijon mustard, mayonnaise and white vinegar. Set aside.
2. Peel the eggs and chop them. Then in a large bowl, mix the shredded cabbage, chopped parsley and chopped eggs.
3. Stir in the prepared dressing and combine well. Season with salt, pepper and poppy seeds.
4. Put it into the refrigerator, for about one hour, before serving. Serve cold and enjoy!

Nutrition Info (Per Serving): 167 Calories; 13g Fat; 6.8g Carbs; 2.5g Fiber; 6.8g Protein

Traditional Spinach and Feta Frittata

Servings: 4

Cooking Time: 40 minutes

Ingredients

- 5 ounces spinach
- 8 ounces crumbled feta cheese
- 1 pint halved cherry tomatoes
- 10 eggs
- 3 tbsp olive oil
- 4 scallions, diced
- Salt and black pepper, to taste

Directions:

1. Preheat your oven to 350° F.

2. Drizzle the oil in a casserole and place in the oven until heated. In a bowl, whisk the eggs along with the black pepper and salt until thoroughly combined. Stir in the spinach, feta cheese, and scallions.

3. Pour the mixture into the casserole, top with the cherry tomatoes and place back in the oven. Bake for 25 minutes until your frittata is set in the middle.

4. When done, remove the casserole from the oven and run a spatula around the edges of the frittata; slide it onto a warm platter. Cut the frittata into wedges and serve with salad.

Nutrition Info (Per Serving): Kcal 461, Fat: 35g, Net Carbs: 6g, Protein: 26g

Italian-style Keto Sandwiches
Servings: 2

Cooking Time: 10 minutes

Ingredients

- 1 tablespoon butter
- 2 eggs
- 4 thin zucchini slices, cut lengthwise
- 2 slices provolone cheese
- 2 slices Genoa salami
- 2 slices Sopressata
- 1 red bell pepper, sliced thinly
- 1 and a half teaspoon chipotle in adobo sauce, minced
- 1 clove garlic, minced
- 2 basil leaves, snipped
- Sea salt and black pepper, to taste

Directions:

1. Melt the butter into a nonstick skillet over medium-high heat. Now, crack the eggs and cook until they are set about 4 to 5 minutes.

2. Place one zucchini slice on two plates. Add the cheese, Genoa Salami, Sopressata, peppers, and garlic to each of the zucchini slices.

4. Top with the fried eggs; sprinkle with basil, salt, and pepper and top with the remaining zucchini slices. Enjoy!

Nutrition Info (Per Serving): 352 Calories; 26.5g Fat; 6.6g Total Carbs; 22.1g Protein; 0.6g Fiber

Spinach and Eggs Salad

Servings: 4

Cooking Time: 0 minutes

Ingredients

- 2 cups baby spinach
- 1 cup cherry tomatoes, cubed
- 1 tablespoon chives, chopped
- 4 eggs, hard-boiled, peeled and roughly cubed
- Salt and black pepper to the taste
- 1 tablespoon lime juice
- 1 tablespoon olive oil

Directions:

1. Combine the spinach with the tomatoes and the other ingredients, toss and serve for breakfast right away.

Nutrition Info: calories 107, fat 8, fiber 0.9, carbs 3.6, protein 6.4

Curried Deviled Eggs

Servings: 2

Cooking Time: 0 minutes

Ingredients

- 2 eggs, boiled
- ¼ tsp curry powder
- 1/8 tsp cayenne pepper
- ½ tsp mustard paste
- 1 ½ tbsp yogurt
- Seasoning:
- 1/8 tsp salt

Directions:

1. Peel the boiled eggs, then slice in half lengthwise and transfer egg yolks to a medium bowl by using a spoon.

2. Mash the egg yolk, add remaining ingredients and stir until well combined.

3. Spoon the egg yolk mixture into egg whites and then serve.

Nutrition Info: 91 Calories; 5.7 g Fats; 7.4 g Protein; 0.8 g Net Carb; 0 g Fiber;

SOUP AND STEWS

Red Gazpacho

Servings: 6

Cooking Time: 10 Min

Ingredients

- 2 green peppers, roasted
- 2 large red peppers, roasted
- 2 avocados, flesh scoped out
- 2 garlic cloves
- 2 spring onions, chopped
- 1 cucumber, chopped
- 1 cup olive oil
- 2 tbsp lemon juice
- 4 tomatoes, chopped
- 7 ounces goat cheese
- 1 red onion, coarsely chopped
- 2 tbsp apple cider vinegar

Directions:

1. Place peppers, tomatoes, avocado, spring onions, garlic, lemon juice, oil, vinegar, and salt in a food processor.
2. Pulse until slightly chunky, but smooth.
3. Adjust the seasoning and transfer to a pot. Stir in cucumbers and red onion.
4. Cover and chill in the fridge for 2 hours.

5. Serve very cold, topped with goat cheese and a drizzle of olive oil.

Nutrition Info (Per Serving): Cal 528; Net Carbs 8.5g; Fat 46g, Protein 7g

Tomato & Basil Soup

Servings: 8

Cooking Time: 28 minutes

Ingredients

- 3 tablespoons olive oil
- 2 small yellow onions, thinly sliced
- Salt, to taste
- 3 teaspoons curry powder
- 1 teaspoon ground cumin
- 1 teaspoon ground coriander
- ½ teaspoon red pepper flakes, crushed
- 1 14-ounces can sugar-free diced tomatoes with juice
- 1 28-ounces can sugar-free plum tomatoes with juices
- 5½ cups homemade vegetable broth
- ¼ cup fresh basil leaves, chopped

Directions:

1. Heat the oil in a large Dutch oven over medium-low heat and cook the onion with one teaspoon of salt for about -12 minutes, stirring occasionally.

2. Stir in the spices and sauté for about 1 minute.

3. Add both cans of tomatoes alongside the juices and broth and stir to combine.

4. Increase the heat to medium-high and cook until boiling.

5. Reduce the heat to medium-low, then simmer for about 1minutes.

6. Remove from the heat and with a hand blender, blend the soup until smooth. Top with fresh basil and serve.

Nutrition Info (Per Serving): Calories: 113; Net Carbs: 2.7g; Carbohydrate: 9.4g; Fiber: 6.7g; Protein: 5.1g; Fat: 6.7g; Sugar: 5.5g; Sodium: 553mg

Salsa Verde Chicken Soup

Servings: 4

Cooking Time: 15 minutes

Ingredients

- ½ cup salsa verde
- 2 cups cooked and shredded chicken
- 2 cups chicken broth
- 1 cup shredded cheddar cheese
- 4 ounces cream cheese
- ½ tsp chili powder
- ½ tsp ground cumin
- ½ tsp fresh cilantro, chopped
- Salt and black pepper, to taste

Directions:

1. Combine the cream cheese, salsa verde, and broth in a food processor; pulse until smooth. Transfer the mixture into a pot, then place over medium heat. Cook until hot, but do not bring to a boil. Add chicken, chili powder, and cumin and cook for about 3-5 minutes, or until it is heated through.

2. Stir in cheddar cheese and season with salt and pepper to taste. If it is very thick, add a few tablespoons of water and boil for 1-3 more minutes. Serve hot in bowls sprinkled with fresh cilantro.

Nutrition Info (Per Serving): Kcal 346, Fat: 23g, Net Carbs: 3g, Protein: 25g

Broccoli Soup

Servings: 5

Cooking Time: 15 minutes

Ingredients

- 4 cups homemade chicken broth
- 20 ounces small broccoli florets
- 12 ounces cheddar cheese, cubed
- Salt and ground black pepper, as required
- 1 cup heavy cream

Directions:

1. In a large soup pan, add the broth and broccoli over medium-high heat and bring to a boil.
2. Reduce the heat to low and simmer, covered for about 5-7 minutes.
3. Stir in the cheese and cook for about 2-minutes, stirring continuously.
4. Stir in the salt, black pepper, and cream and cook for about 2 minutes.
5. Serve hot.

Nutrition Info (Per Serving): Calories: 426; Net Carbs: 6g; Carbohydrate: 9g; Fiber: 3g; Protein: 24.5g; Fat: 32.9g; Sugar: 2.9g; Sodium: 1000mg

Cauliflower Soup with Kielbasa

Servings: 4

Cooking Time: 40 minutes

Ingredients

- 1 cauliflower head, chopped
- 1 rutabaga, chopped
- 3 tbsp ghee
- 1 kielbasa sausage, sliced
- 2 cups chicken broth
- 1 small onion, chopped
- 2 cups of water
- Salt and black pepper, to taste

Directions:

1. Melt 2 tbsp of the ghee into a pot and cook the onion for 3 minutes. Add cauliflower and rutabaga, and cook for another 5 minutes. Pour broth, water, salt, and pepper over. Bring to a boil, then cook for 20 minutes.
1. Melt remaining butter in a skillet. Add in kielbasa sausage and cook for 5 minutes. Puree the soup until smooth. Serve with kielbasa.

Nutrition Info (Per Serving): Cal 251; Net Carbs: 5.7g; Fat: 19g, Protein: 10g

Bacon Stew with Cauliflower

Servings: 6

Cooking Time: 40 minutes

- **Ingredients**
- 1 head cauliflower, cut into florets
- 8 oz grated mozzarella
- 2 cups chicken broth
- ½ tsp garlic powder
- ½ tsp onion powder
- Salt and black pepper, to taste
- 4 garlic cloves, minced
- ¼ cup heavy cream
- 3 cups bacon, chopped

Directions:

1. In a pot, combine the bacon with broth, cauliflower, salt, heavy cream, black pepper, garlic powder, cheese, onion powder, and garlic, and cook for 35 minutes. Serve.

Nutrition Info (Per Serving): Cal 380; Net Carbs 6g; Fat 25g; Protein 33g

MAIN

Zucchini Noodle Carbonara

Servings: 2

Cooking Time: 10 minutes

Ingredients

- 2 large zucchini
- 1 large egg
- 1 egg yolk
- ¼ cup grated cheddar cheese
- 3 slices of turkey bacon, diced

- Seasoning:
- 1/4 tsp sea salt
- 1/2 tsp fresh ground black pepper

Directions:

1. Prepare zucchini noodles, and for this, cut off the bottom and top of zucchini and then use a spiralizer to convert them into noodles.

2. Take a baking sheet, line it with a paper towel, then lay the zucchini noodles on them, sprinkle with salt, and let sit for 5 minutes. Then wrap zucchini noodles in a cheesecloth and squeeze well to remove its liquid as much as possible and set aside until required.

3. Prepare the sauce and for this, crack the egg in a bowl, add egg yolk and cheese and whisk until well combined. Take a skillet pan, place it over medium heat, add bacon slices,

and cook for 3 to 5 minutes until crispy. Then add zucchini noodles and cook for 3 minutes until warmed through. Switch heat to a low level, pour in egg mixture, stir well and remove the pan from heat. Stir the zucchini noodle until the egg is just cooked and then sprinkle with black pepper

4. Serve.

Nutrition Info: 114 Calories; 7 g Fats; 8 g Protein; 1.5 g Net Carb; 1.5 g Fiber

Radish & Zucchini Quiche

Servings: 4

Preparation Time: 10 minutes

Cooking Time: 45 minutes

Ingredients:

- Zucchini -blanched, chopped - 1
- Garlic cloves -sliced thinly: 2
- Eggs - 8
- Coconut cream: ½ cup
- Fresh herbs -thyme, tarragon, rosemary: 1 bunch
- Sea salt: 4 ½ teaspoon
- Radishes -cubed: ½ pound
- Black pepper -ground: ½ teaspoon
- Coconut oil for frying

Directions:

1. Heat the coconut oil in a skillet and sauté the garlic and zucchini in it for 5 minutes.
2. Whisk together the coconut cream, eggs, and a pinch of salt.
3. Place the radish and zucchini into a pie dish greased with cooking spray and pour the egg over.
4. Bake for 45 minutes at 325 degrees Fahrenheit until it begins to brown on top.

Nutrition Value:

248 Cal, 19.4 g total fat -11.1 g sat. fat, 336 mg chol., 2264 mg sodium, 7.6 g carbs, 2.6g fiber, 13.3 g protein.

Quattro Formaggi Pizza

Servings: 4

Cooking Time: 15 minutes

Ingredients

- 1 tbsp olive oil
- ½ cup cheddar cheese, shredded
- 1 ¼ cups mozzarella cheese, shredded
- ½ cup mascarpone cheese
- ½ cup blue cheese
- 2 tbsp sour cream
- 2 garlic cloves, chopped
- 1 red bell pepper, sliced
- 1 green bell pepper, sliced
- 10 cherry tomatoes, halved
- 1 tsp oregano
- Salt and black pepper, to taste

Directions:

1. In a bowl, mix the cheeses. Set a pan over medium heat, then warm olive oil.
2. Spread the cheese mixture on the pan and cook for 5 minutes until cooked through.
3. Scatter garlic and sour cream over the crust.
4. Add in tomatoes and bell peppers; cook for 2 minutes.
5. Sprinkle with pepper, salt and oregano and serve.

Nutrition Info (Per Serving): Kcal 266, Fat: 23.6g, Net Carbs: 6.6g, Protein: 9g

Keto Soufflé with Chorizo Sausage
Servings: 8

Cooking Time: 55 minutes

Ingredients

- 8 ounces Chorizo sausage, sliced
- 4 scallions, chopped
- 1 red bell pepper, chopped
- 4 garlic cloves, minced
- Kosher salt, black pepper to taste
- 1/2 teaspoon cayenne pepper
- 8 ounces cream cheese
- 4 tablespoons milk
- 10 eggs
- 1 cup Swiss cheese, grated

Directions:

1. Preheat an oven-safe skillet over medium-high heat. Then cook the sausage for 5 to 6 minutes, crumbling it with a spatula.

2. Add in the scallions, peppers, and garlic and continue to sauté for an additional minute. Now season with salt, black pepper, and cayenne pepper.

3. In a mixing bowl, thoroughly combine the cream cheese, eggs, and milk. Pour the egg mixture into the pan and shake the pan to spread it evenly.

4. Transfer the pan to the oven and then bake at 370 degrees F for about 28 minutes or until cooked through.

5. Top with the Swiss cheese and broil your souffle for 6 minutes more or until the cheese is bubbling. Bon appétit!

Nutrition Info (Per Serving): 348 Calories; 28.7g Fat; 4.5g Carbs; 17.6g Protein; 0.3g Fiber

Vodka Cauliflower Casserole

Servings: 8

Preparation Time: 10 minutes

Cooking Time: 30 minutes

Ingredients:

- Cauliflower florets -cooked, drained: 8 cups
- Vodka sauce: 2 cups
- Heavy whipping cream: 2 tablespoon
- Butter -melted: 2 tablespoon
- Parmesan cheese -grated: 1/3 cup
- Kosher salt: ½ teaspoon
- Black pepper -ground: ¼ teaspoon
- Provolone cheese: 6 slices
- Fresh basil -chopped: ¼ cup

Directions:

1. Mix together all the ingredients except the basil and Provolone cheese.
2. Transfer the mixture into a baking pan and place the Provolone cheese slices on top.
3. Bake for 30-40 minutes in an oven preheated to 375 degrees
1. Fahrenheit until the cheese has melted and the casserole bubbles.
4. Remove and leave aside for 10 minutes.
5. Serve garnished with the basil.

Nutrition Value:

214 Cal, 14 g total fat, 6 g net carbs, 12 g protein.

MEAT

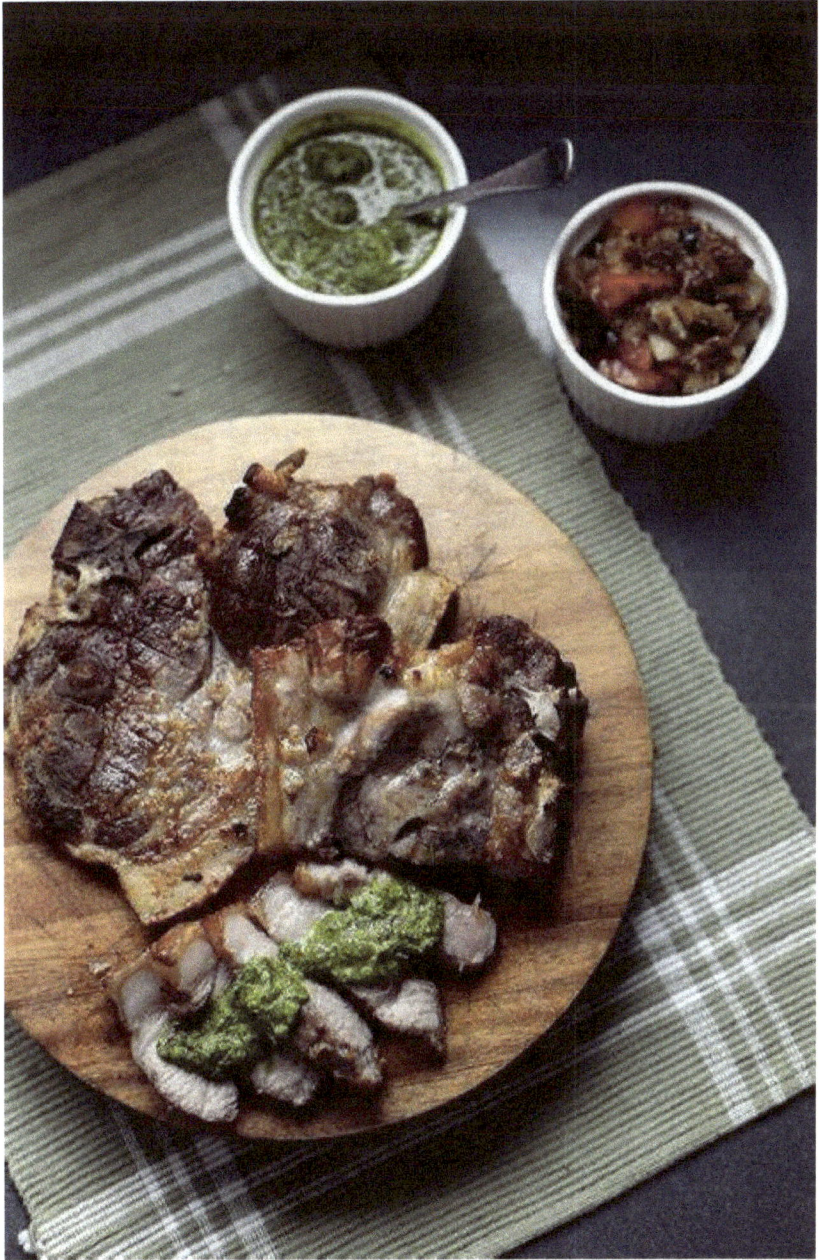

Pork with Olives

Servings: 4

Cooking Time: 30 minutes

Ingredients

- 1 pound pork stew meat, cubed
- 2 tablespoons ghee, melted
- 1 red onion, chopped
- 1 cup beef stock
- 1 cup black olives, pitted and halved
- A pinch of salt and black pepper
- 2 garlic cloves, minced
- 1 tablespoon oregano, chopped

Directions:

1. Heat up a pan with the ghee over medium heat, add the onion and the meat and brown for 5 minutes.
2. Add the rest of the ingredients, toss, cook over medium heat for minutes more, divide into bowls and serve.

Nutrition Info: calories 165, fat 2, fiber 1, carbs 2, protein 26

Szechuan Beef Stir Fry

Servings: 4

Cooking Time: 20 minutes

Ingredients

- 2 tablespoons sesame oil
- 1 ½ pounds shoulder top blade, cut into strips
- 1 shallot, sliced
- 1 teaspoon ginger-garlic paste
- 3 teaspoons tamari sauce

Directions:

1. Heat the sesame oil in a wok over a moderate flame. Now, fry the beef for 4 to 6 minutes, frequently stirring, until browned; reserve.

2. Now, stir in the shallot and ginger garlic paste and continue cooking for an additional 3 minutes or until they are fragrant. Add back the reserved beef.

3. Add in the tamari sauce and stir for 5 minutes more to coat the beef with the sauce. Transfer your stir fry to serving plates and garnish with toasted sesame seeds, if desired. Enjoy!

Nutrition Info (Per Serving): 302 Calories; 16.6g Fat; 3.7g Carbs; 35.2g Protein; 0.7g Fiber

Savory Pork Tacos

Servings: 4

Cooking Time: 7 Hours

Ingredients

- 2 tbsp olive oil
- ½ cup sliced yellow onion
- 2 lb pork shoulder
- 4 tbsp ras el hanout seasoning
- Salt to taste
- 3 ½ cups beef broth
- 5 tbsp psyllium husk powder
- 1 ¼ cups almond flour
- 2 eggs, cracked into a bowl
- 2 tbsp butter, for frying

Directions:

1. In a pot, heat olive oil and sauté onion for 3 minutes or until softened. Season pork shoulder with ras el hanout, salt, and place in the onion. Sear on each side for 3 minutes and pour the broth on top. Cover the lid, reduce heat to low, and cook for 4 to 5 hours or until the pork softens. Shred the pork with two forks. Cook further over low heat for an hour; set aside. In a bowl, combine psyllium husk powder, almond flour, and 1 tsp of salt. Mix in eggs until a thick dough forms and add 1 cup of water.

2. Separate the dough into 8 pieces. Lay a parchment paper on a flat surface, grease with cooking spray, and put a dough piece on top. Cover with another parchment paper and, using a rolling pin, flatten the dough into a circle. Repeat the same process for the remaining dough balls. Melt a quarter of the butter in a skillet over and fry the flattened dough one after another on both sides until light brown, 40 minutes in total. Transfer the keto tortillas to plates, spoon shredded meat and serve.

Nutrition Info (Per Serving): Cal 520; Net Carbs 3.8g; Fat 30g; Protein 50g

Roasted Spicy Beef

Servings: 4

Cooking Time: 70 minutes

Ingredients

- 2 lb beef brisket
- ½ tsp celery salt
- 1 tsp chili powder
- 1 tbsp avocado oil
- 1 tbsp sweet paprika
- A pinch of cayenne pepper
- ½ tsp garlic powder
- ½ cup beef stock
- 1 tbsp garlic, minced
- ¼ tsp dry mustard

Directions:

1. Preheat oven to 340°F. In a bowl, combine the paprika with dry mustard, chili powder, salt, garlic powder, cayenne pepper, and celery salt. Rub the meat with this mixture.

2. Set a pan over medium heat and warm avocado oil, place in the beef, and sear until brown. Remove to a baking dish. Pour in the stock, add garlic and bake for 60 minutes.

3. Set the beef to a cutting board, leave to cool before slicing and splitting in serving plates. Take the juices from the baking dish and strain, sprinkle over the meat, and enjoy.

Nutrition Info (Per Serving): Kcal 480, Fat 23.5g, Net Carbs 3.5g, Protein 55g

Delicious Sausage Salad

Servings: 4

Cooking Time: 7 minutes

Ingredients

- 8 pork sausage links, sliced
- 1 pound mixed cherry tomatoes, cut in halves
- 4 cups baby spinach
- 1 tablespoon avocado oil
- 1 pound mozzarella cheese, cubed
- 2 tablespoons lemon juice
- 2/3 cup basil pesto
- Salt and black pepper to the taste

Directions:

1. Heat up a pan with the oil over medium-high heat, add sausage slices, stir and cook them for 4 minutes on each side.
2. Meanwhile, in a salad bowl, mix spinach with mozzarella, tomatoes, salt, pepper, lemon juice, pesto, and toss to coat.
3. Add sausage pieces, toss again and serve.
4. Enjoy!

Nutrition Info: calories 250, fat 12, fiber 3, carbs 8, protein 18

Beef Shanks Braised in Red Wine Sauce

Preparation Time: 20 minutes

Cooking Time: 8 hrs.

Servings: 6

Ingredients:

- 2 tablespoons olive oil
- pounds (907 g) beef shanks
- 2 cups dry red wine
- cups beef stock
- 1 sprig of fresh rosemary
- 5 garlic cloves, finely chopped
- 1 onion, finely chopped
- Pepper and salt

Directions:

1. Heat olive oil.
2. Put the beef shanks into the skillet and fry for 5 to 10 minutes until well browned.
3. The beef shanks halfway through. Set aside.
4. The red wine must be poured into the pot and let simmer.
5. Add the cooked beef shanks, dry red wine, beef stock, rosemary, garlic, onion, salt, and black pepper to the slow cooker. Stir to mix well.
6. Slow cook with the lid on for 8 hrs.

Nutrition:

Calories: 341 Fat: 19.6g Fiber: 10 g Carbohydrates:15.4 g Protein: 21.6g

Herbed Grilled Lamb

Preparation Time: 15 minutes

Cooking Time: 20 minutes

Servings: 6

Ingredients:

- 2 pounds of lamb
- 5 spoons of ghee butter
- 3 tablespoons of Keto mustard
- 2 minced garlic cloves
- 1 1/2 tablespoon of chopped basil
- 1/2 tablespoon of pepper
- 3 tablespoons of olive oil
- 1/2 teaspoon of salt

Directions:

1. Mix butter, mustard, and basil with a pinch of salt to taste. Then, set aside.
2. Mix garlic, salt, and pepper together. Then, add a teaspoon of oil. Season the lamb generously with this mix.
3. Grill the lamb on medium heat until fully cooked.
4. Take butter mix and spread generously on chops and serve hot.

Nutrition:

Calories: 390 Fat: 19.5 g Fiber: 5.9g Carbohydrates: 3.2 g Protein: 18.6 g

Coconut and Lime Steak

Preparation Time: 25 minutes

Cooking Time: 15 minutes

Servings: 4

Ingredients:

- 2 pounds steak, grass-fed
- 1 tablespoon minced garlic
- 1 lime, zested
- 1 teaspoon ginger, grated
- 3/4 teaspoon sea salt
- 1 teaspoon red pepper flakes
- 2 tablespoons lime juice
- 1/2 cup coconut oil, melted

Directions:

1. Take a large bowl and add garlic, ginger, salt, red pepper flakes, lime juice, zest, pour in oil, and whisk until combined.
2. Add the steaks, toss until well coated, and marinate at room temperature for 20 minutes.
3. After 20 minutes, take a large skillet pan, place it over medium-high heat, and when hot, add steaks (cut steaks in half if they don't fit into the pan).
4. Cook the steaks and then transfer them to a cutting board.

5. Let steaks cool for 5 minutes, then slice across the grain and serve.

Nutrition:

Calories: 512 Fat: 17.9g Fiber: 12.5g Carbohydrates: 4.9 g Protein: 19.9g

POULTRY

Almond Crusted Chicken Zucchini Stacks

Servings: 4

Cooking Time: 30 minutes

Ingredients

- 1 ½ lb chicken thighs, skinless and boneless, cut into strips
- 3 tbsp almond flour
- Salt and black pepper to taste
- 2 large zucchinis, sliced
- 4 tbsp olive oil
- 2 tsp Italian mixed herb blend
- ½ cup chicken broth

Directions:

1. Preheat oven to 400° F. In a zipper bag, add almond flour, salt, and pepper. Mix and add the chicken slices. Seal the bag and shake to coat.

2. Arrange the zucchinis on a greased baking sheet.

3. Season with salt and pepper, and drizzle with 2 tbsp of olive oil. Remove the chicken from the almond flour mixture, shake off, and put 2-3 chicken strips on each zucchini. Season with an herb blend and drizzle again with olive oil. Bake for 8 minutes; remove the sheet and pour in broth. Bake further for minutes. Serve warm.

Nutrition Info (Per Serving): Cal 512; Net Carbs 1.2g; Fat 42g; Protein 29g

So Delicious Chicken Wings

Servings: 4

Cooking Time: 55 minutes

Ingredients

- 3 pounds of chicken wings
- Salt and black pepper to the taste
- 3 tablespoons coconut aminos
- 2 teaspoons white vinegar
- 3 tablespoons rice vinegar
- 3 tablespoons stevia
- ¼ cup scallions, chopped
- ½ teaspoon xantham gum
- 5 dried chilies, chopped

Directions:

1. Spread chicken wings on a lined baking sheet, season with salt and pepper, introduce in the oven at 375 degrees F and bake for 45 minutes.

2. Meanwhile, heat up a small pan over medium heat, add white vinegar, rice vinegar, coconut aminos, stevia, xantham gum, scallions and chilies, stir well, bring to a boil, cook for minutes and take off the heat.

3. Dip chicken wings into this sauce, arrange them all on the baking sheet again and bake for 10 minutes more.

4. Serve them hot.

5. Enjoy!

Nutrition Info: calories 415, fat 23, fiber 3, carbs 2, protein 27

Chicken and Mushrooms

Servings: 4

Cooking Time: 30 minutes

Ingredients

- 1 pound chicken breast, skinless, boneless and cubed
- 2 cups baby bella mushrooms, sliced
- 2 tablespoons olive oil
- 1 red onion, chopped
- 1 red bell pepper, chopped
- 2 garlic cloves, minced
- A pinch of salt and black pepper
- ½ cup chicken stock
- 1 tablespoon balsamic vinegar
- 1 tablespoon parsley, chopped

Directions:

1. Heat up a pan with the oil over medium heat, add the onion and the mushrooms, stir and cook for 5 minutes.
2. Add the chicken, toss and brown for 5 minutes more.
3. Add the rest of the ingredients, toss, bring to a simmer and cook over medium heat for 20 minutes.
4. Divide everything between plates and serve.

Nutrition Info: calories 340, fat 33, fiber 3, carbs 4, protein 20

Creamy Chicken Thighs with Capers
Servings: 4

Cooking Time: 30 minutes

Ingredients

- 2 tbsp butter
- 1 ½ lb chicken thighs
- 2 cups crème fraîche
- 8 oz cream cheese
- 1/3 cup capers
- 1 tbsp tamari sauce

Directions:

1. Heat oven to 350° F and grease a baking sheet. Melt butter in a skillet, season the chicken with salt and pepper and fry until golden brown, 8 minutes.

2. Transfer chicken to the baking sheet, cover with aluminum foil and bake for 8 minutes. Reserve the butter used to sear the chicken.

3. Remove chicken from the oven, take off the foil, and pour the drippings into a pan along with the butter from frying. Set the chicken aside in a warmer for Serves. Place the saucepan over low heat and mix in crème Fraiche and cream cheese.

4. Simmer until the sauce thickens.

5. Mix in capers and tamari sauce; cook further for a minute, and season with salt and pepper. Dish the chicken into plates and drizzle the sauce all over. Serve with buttered broccoli.

Nutrition Info (Per Serving): Cal 834; Net Carbs 0.9g; Fat 73g; Protein 36g

FISH

Pistachio-crusted Salmon

Servings: 4

Cooking Time: 35 minutes

Ingredients

- 4 salmon fillets
- ½ tsp pepper
- 1 tsp salt
- ¼ cup mayonnaise
- ½ cup chopped pistachios

Sauce:

- 1 chopped shallot
- 2 tsp lemon zest
- 1 tbsp olive oil
- A pinch of black pepper
- 1 cup heavy cream

Directions:

1. Preheat the oven to 370° F.

2. Brush the salmon with mayonnaise and season with salt and pepper. Coat with pistachios, place in a lined baking dish and bake for 15 minutes.

3. Heat olive oil in a saucepan and sauté the shallot for minutes. Stir in the rest of the sauce ingredients. Bring the mixture to a boil and cook until thickened. Serve the fish with the sauce.

Nutrition Info (Per Serving): Kcal 563, Fat: 47g, Net Carbs: 6g, Protein: 34g

Cod Fillets with Tangy Sesame Sauce

Servings: 6

Cooking Time: 15 minutes

Ingredients

- 6 cod fillets, skin-on
- 3 tablespoons olive oil
- Sea salt and ground black pepper, to season
- 1 lemon, freshly squeezed
- 1/2 teaspoon fresh ginger, minced
- 1 garlic clove, minced
- 1 red chili pepper, minced
- 3 tablespoons toasted sesame seeds
- 3 tablespoons toasted sesame oil

Directions:

1. Prepare a grill for medium-high heat. Rub the cod fillets with olive oil; season both sides with salt and black pepper.
2. Next, place the cod fillets on the grill skin side down. Grill approximately 7 minutes until the skin is lightly charred.
3. To make the sauce, whisk the remaining ingredients until well combined; season with lots of black pepper.
4. Divide the cod fillets among serving plates. Spoon the sauce over them and enjoy!

Nutrition Info (Per Serving): 341 Calories; 17g Fat; 3.2g Carbs; 42.1g Protein; 0.9g Fiber

Fried Salmon with Asparagus

Servings: 3

Cooking Time: 25 Minute

Ingredients

- 1 cup green asparagus, trimmed
- 2 cloves garlic, sliced
- sea salt and pepper, to taste
- 1 lb salmon fillet, cut into pieces
- 2 tablespoons salted butter
- 2 tablespoons avocado oil
- lemon wedges, optional

Directions:

1. In a medium saucepan, heat the avocado oil. Add the asparagus and garlic. Cook for 5-6 minutes. Season with sea salt and pepper. Set aside.

2. Heat the salted butter in a large skillet. Place the salmon pieces in the skillet.

3. Season with sea salt and pepper. Cook for 4 minutes per side or until cooked through.

4. Serve hot with fresh lemon wedges. Enjoy!

Nutrition Info (Per Serving): 381 Calories; 25g Fat; 4.9g Carbs; 1.3 Fibers; 32.6g Protein

Shrimp Wraps

Servings: 2

Cooking Time: 10 minutes

Ingredients

- 4 oz shrimps
- 2 tbsp coconut flour
- ½ tsp garlic powder
- 1 tbsp avocado oil
- 2 cabbage leaves

Seasoning:

- ¼ tsp salt
- 1/8 tsp ground black pepper
- 1 tbsp water
- 2 tbsp mayonnaise

Directions:

1. Take a shallow dish, place coconut flour in it, and then stir in garlic, powder, salt, and black pepper.

2. Stir in water until smooth and then coat each shrimp in it, one at a time. Take a medium skillet pan, place it over medium heat, add oil and when hot, add shrimps in it and cook for 3 minutes per side until cooked.

3. Distribute shrimps between two cabbage leaves, drizzle with mayonnaise, then roll like a wrap and serve.

Nutrition Info: 265 Calories; 19.9 g Fats; 13.6 g Protein; 3.2 g Net Carb; 3.3 g Fiber

Catfish & Cauliflower Casserole

Servings: 4

Cooking Time: 30 minutes

Ingredients

- 1 tablespoon sesame oil
- 11 ounces cauliflower
- 4 scallions
- 1 garlic clove, minced
- 1 teaspoon fresh ginger root, grated
- Salt and ground black pepper, to taste
- Cayenne pepper, to taste
- 2 sprigs dried thyme, crushed
- 1 sprig rosemary, crushed
- 24 ounces catfish, cut into pieces
- 1/2 cup cream cheese
- 1/2 cup double cream
- 1 egg
- 2 ounces butter, cold

Directions:

1. Start by preheating your oven to 390 degrees F. Now, lightly grease a casserole dish with a nonstick cooking spray.

2. Then, heat the oil in a pan over medium-high heat; once hot, cook the cauliflower and scallions until tender or 5 to

6 minutes. Add the garlic and ginger; continue to sauté 1 minute more.

3. Transfer the vegetables to the prepared casserole dish. Sprinkle with seasonings. Add catfish to the top.

4. In a mixing bowl, thoroughly combine the cream cheese, double cream, and egg. Spread this creamy mixture over the top of your casserole.

5. Top with slices of butter. Bake in the preheated oven for 18 to 22 minutes or until the fish flakes easily with a fork. Bon appétit!

Nutrition Info (Per Serving): 510 Calories; 40g Fat; 5.5g Carbs; 1.6g Fiber; 31.3g Protein

Trout and Endives

Servings: 2

Cooking Time: 15 minutes

Ingredients

- 4 trout fillets
- 2 endives, shredded
- ½ cup shallots, chopped
- 2 tablespoons olive oil
- 1 teaspoon rosemary, dried
- ¼ cup chicken stock
- A pinch of salt and black pepper
- 2 tablespoons chives, chopped

Directions:

1. Heat up a pan with the oil over medium heat, add the shallots and the endives, toss and cook for 2 minutes.
2. Add the fish and cook it for minutes on each side.
3. Add the rest of the ingredients, cook for 8-9 minutes more, divide between plates and serve.

Nutrition Info: calories 200, fat 5, fiber 2, carbs 2, protein 7

Scallops with Broccoli

Servings: 5

Cooking Time: 10 minutes

Ingredients

For Broccoli:

- 1¼ pounds small broccoli florets
- 2 tablespoons unsalted butter, melted

For Scallops:

- 1 tablespoon butter
- 2 garlic cloves, minced
- 1 pound fresh jumbo scallops, side muscles removed
- Salt and ground black pepper, as required
- 2 tablespoons fresh lemon juice
- 2 scallions green part, thinly sliced

Directions:

1. For the broccoli: arrange a steamer basket in a pan of water over medium-high heat and bring to a boil.

2. Place the broccoli in a steamer basket and steam, covered for about 4-5 minutes.

3. Meanwhile, in a large skillet, melt the butter over medium-high heat and sauté the garlic for about 1 minute.

4. Now, add the scallops and cook for about 2 minutes per side.

5. Stir in the salt, black pepper, and lemon juice and remove from heat.

6. Drain the broccoli and transfer it onto a plate.

7. Drizzle the broccoli evenly with melted butter.

8. Divide the cooked broccoli onto serving plates and top with scallops.

9. Garnish with scallions and serve immediately.

Nutrition Info (Per Serving): Calories: 266; Net Carbs: 5.2g; Carbohydrate: 8.3g; Fiber: 3.1g; Protein: 33.1g; Fat: 8.6g; Sugar: 2.2g; Sodium: 430mg

VEGETABLES

Classic Tangy Ratatouille

Servings: 6

Cooking Time: 47 minutes

Ingredients

- 2 eggplants, chopped
- 3 zucchinis, chopped
- 2 red onions, diced
- 1 (28 oz) can tomatoes
- 2 red bell peppers, cut into chunks
- 1 yellow bell pepper, cut into chunks
- 3 cloves garlic, sliced
- ½ cup basil leaves, chop half
- 4 sprigs thyme
- 1 tbsp balsamic vinegar
- 2 tbsp olive oil
- ½ lemon, zested

Directions:

1. In a casserole pot, heat the olive oil and sauté the eggplants, zucchinis, and bell peppers over medium heat for 5 minutes. Spoon the veggies into a large bowl.

2. In the same pan, sauté garlic, onions, and thyme leaves for 5 minutes and return the cooked veggies to the pan along with the canned tomatoes, balsamic vinegar, chopped

basil, salt, and black pepper to taste. Stir and cover the pot, and cook the ingredients on low heat for 30 minutes.

3. Open the lid and stir in the remaining basil leaves, lemon zest, and adjust the seasoning. Turn the heat off. Plate the ratatouille and serve with some low carb crusted bread.

Nutrition Info (Per Serving): Kcal 154, Fat 12.1g, Net Carbs 5.6g, Protein 1.7g

Garlicky Bok Choy

Servings: 4

Cooking Time: 25 minutes

Ingredients

- 2 pounds bok choy, chopped
- 2 tbsp almond oil
- 1 tsp garlic, minced
- ½ tsp thyme
- ½ tsp red pepper flakes, crushed
- Salt and black pepper, to the taste

Directions:

1. Add bok choy in a pot with salted water and cook for minutes over medium heat. Drain and set aside.

2. Place a sauté pan over medium heat and warm oil. Add in garlic and cook until soft. Stir in the bok choy, red pepper, black pepper, salt, and thyme.

3. Add more seasonings if needed and serve with cauli rice.

Nutrition Info (Per Serving): Kcal 118; Fat: 7g, Net Carbs: 13.4g, Protein: 2.9g

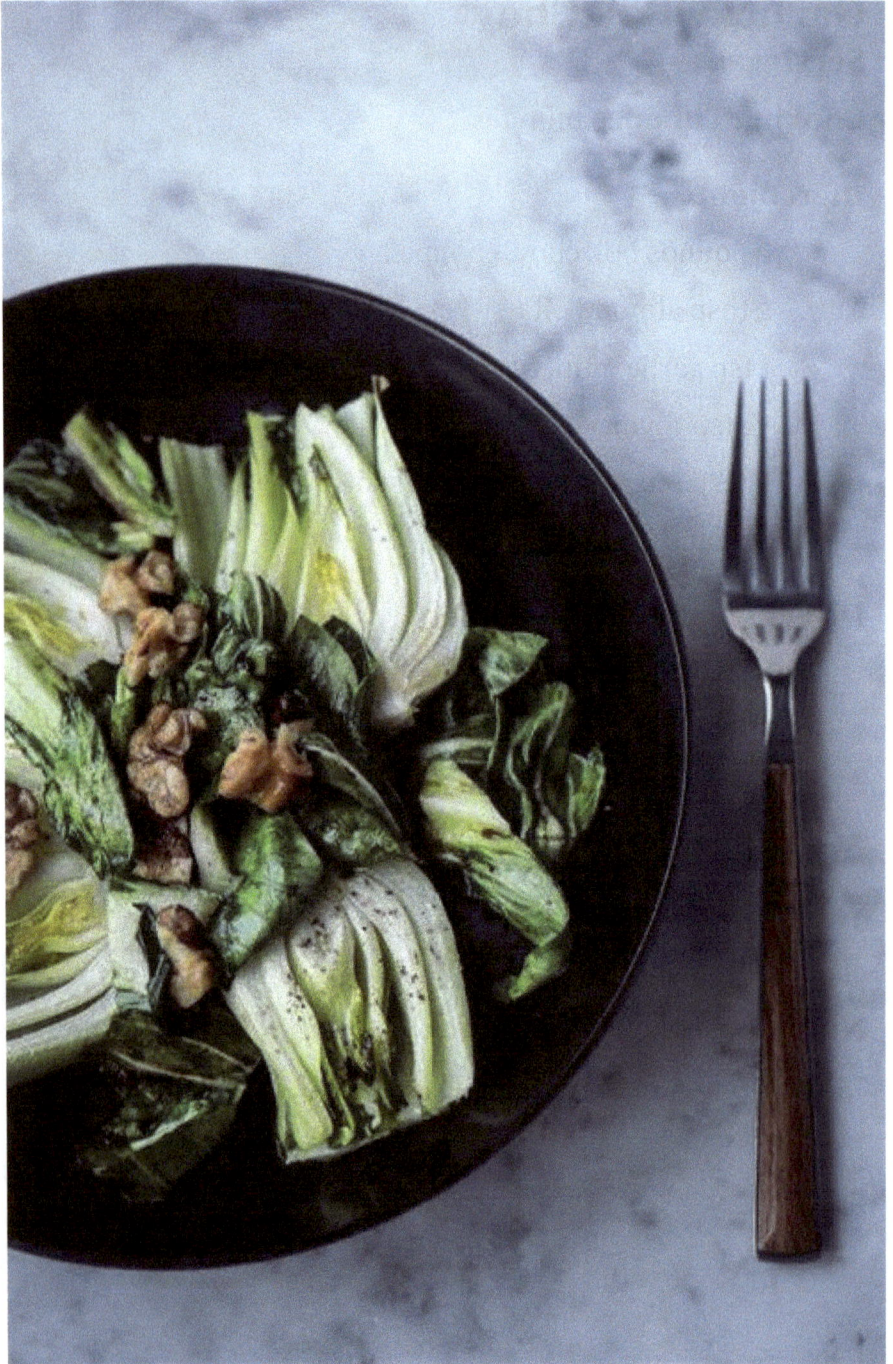

Cheesy Zucchini Bake

Servings: 4

Cooking Time: 25 minutes

Ingredients

- 3 large zucchinis, sliced
- 3 tbsp salted butter, melted
- 2 tbsp olive oil
- 1 garlic clove, minced
- 1 tsp dried thyme
- ¼ cup grated mozzarella
- 2/3 cup grated Parmesan

Directions:

1. Preheat oven to 350° F. Pour zucchini in a bowl; add in butter, olive oil, garlic, and thyme; toss to coat. Spread onto a baking dish and sprinkle with the mozzarella and Parmesan cheeses.

2. Bake for minutes or until the cheese melts and is golden.

3. Serve warm with a garden green salad.

Nutrition Info (Per Serving): Cal 194; Net Carbs 3g; Fat 17.2g; Protein 7.4g

Mixed Veggie Salad

Servings: 4

Cooking Time: 20 minutes

Ingredients

For Dressing:

- 1 small avocado, peeled, pitted and chopped
- ¼ cup plain Greek yogurt
- 1 small yellow onion, chopped
- 1 garlic clove, chopped
- 2 tablespoons fresh parsley
- 2 tablespoons fresh lemon juice

For Salad:

- 6 cups fresh spinach, shredded
- 2 medium zucchinis, cut into thin slices
- ½ cup celery, sliced
- ½ cup red bell pepper, seeded and sliced
- ½ cup yellow onion, thinly sliced
- ½ cup cucumber, thinly sliced
- ½ cup cherry tomatoes halved
- ¼ cup Kalamata olives pitted
- ½ cup feta cheese, crumbled

Directions:

1. For the dressing: in a food processor, add all the ingredients and pulse until smooth. For the salad: in a salad bowl, add all the ingredients and mix well.

2. Place the dressing over salad and gently toss to coat well.

3. Serve immediately.

Nutrition Info (Per Serving): Calories: 148; Net Carbs: 6.3g; Carbohydrate: 10.9g; Fiber: 4.6g; Protein: 5.3g; Fat: 10.3g; Sugar: 4.4g; Sodium: 238mg

Broccoli Slaw Salad with Mustard-mayo Dressing

Servings: 6

Cooking Time: 10 minutes

Ingredients

- 2 tbsp granulated swerve
- 1 tbsp Dijon mustard
- 1 tbsp olive oil
- 4 cups broccoli slaw
- ⅓ cup mayonnaise, sugar-free
- 1 tsp celery seeds
- 1 ½ tbsp apple cider vinegar
- Salt and black pepper, to taste

Directions:

1. Whisk together the ingredients except for the broccoli slaw. Place broccoli slaw in a large salad bowl. Pour the dressing over. Mix with your hands to combine well.

Nutrition Info (Per Serving): Kcal 110, Fat: 10g, Net Carbs: 2g, Protein: 3g

DESSERT

Simple Chocolate Tart

Servings: 4

Cooking Time: 25 minutes

Ingredients

For the crust:

- 1 1/3 cups almond flour
- 1 ½ tsp coconut flour
- ¼ cup swerve sugar
- 1 ½ tsp cold water
- 3 tbsp cold butter

For the filling:
- 4 oz heavy cream
- 4 oz dark chocolate chips
- 1/3 cup erythritol

Directions:

1. Preheat oven to 350° F. In a food processor, blend almond and coconut flours, swerve, water, and butter until smooth. Spread the dough in a greased round baking pan and bake for minutes; let cool.

2. For the filling, heat heavy cream and chocolate chips in a pot over medium heat until chocolate melts; whisk in erythritol.

3. Pour the filling into the crust, gently tap on a flat surface to release air bubbles and chill for 1 hour.

4. Remove from the fridge, and serve.

Nutrition Info (Per Serving): Cal 177; Net Carbs 1g; Fat 19g; Protein 3g

Chocolate Chip Blondies

Servings: 2

Cooking Time: 30 minutes

Ingredients

- 1/2 cup almond flour
- 1/4 teaspoon cream of tartar
- 1/4 teaspoon baking soda
- A pinch of salt
- A pinch of grated nutmeg
- 1 egg, whisked
- 1/4 cup butter, melted
- 1 tablespoon milk
- 1/2 cup Swerve sweetener
- 1/2 teaspoon vanilla bean seeds
- 1/4 cup chocolate chips, unsweetened

Directions:

1. In a mixing bowl, thoroughly combine the almond flour, cream of tartar, baking soda, salt, and nutmeg. In another bowl, whisk the egg, butter, milk, and sweetener.

2. Add the almond flour mixture to the egg mixture and mix to combine well. Afterwards, stir in the vanilla bean seeds and chocolate chips; stir again using a spatula.

3. Scrape the batter into a parchment-lined baking pan. Bake in the preheated oven at 0 degrees F for 22 to 25 minutes. Don't over-bake; the blondies should remain juicy in the center.

4. Let it cool down; then, cut into equal size squares and enjoy!

Nutrition Info (Per Serving): 347 Calories; 34g Fat; 5.2g Total Carbs; 5.7g Protein; 2.8g Fiber

Strawberry Stew

Servings: 4

Cooking Time: 15 minutes

Ingredients

- ½ cup swerve
- 1 pound strawberries, halved
- 2 cups of water
- 1 teaspoon vanilla extract

Directions:

1. In a pan, combine the strawberries with the swerve and the other ingredients, toss gently, bring to a simmer and cook over medium heat for minutes.
2. Divide into bowls and serve cold.

Nutrition Info: calories 40, fat 4.3, fiber 2.3, carbs 3.4, protein 0.8

Passion Fruit Cheesecake Slices

Servings: 8

Cooking Time: 15 minutes + Cooling Time

Ingredients

- 1 cup crushed almond biscuits
- ½ cup melted butter Filling:
- 1 ½ cups cream cheese
- ¾ cup swerve sugar
- 1 ½ whipping cream
- 1 tsp vanilla bean paste
- 4-6 tbsp cold water
- 1 tbsp gelatin powder

Passionfruit jelly:

- 1 cup passion fruit pulp
- ¼ cup swerve confectioner's sugar
- 1 tsp gelatin powder
- ¼ cup water, room temperature

Directions:

1. Mix the crushed biscuits and butter in a bowl, spoon into a spring-form pan, and use the spoon's back to level at the bottom. Set aside in the fridge. Put the cream cheese, swerve sugar, and vanilla paste into a bowl, and use the hand mixer to whisk until smooth; set aside.

2. In a bowl, add tbsp of cold water and sprinkle 1 tbsp of gelatin powder. Let dissolve for 5 minutes. Pour the gelatin liquid along with the whipping cream in the cheese mixture and fold gently.

3. Remove the spring-form pan from the refrigerator and pour over the mixture. Return to the fridge.

4. For the passionfruit jelly: add 2 tbsp of cold water and sprinkle 1 tsp of gelatin powder. Let dissolve for 5 minutes. Pour the confectioner's sugar and ¼ cup of water into it.

5. Mix and stir in passion fruit pulp.

6. Remove the cake again and pour the jelly over it. Swirl the pan to make the jelly level up. Place the pan back into the fridge to cool for 2 hours. When completely set, remove and unlock the spring-pan. Lift the pan from the cake and slice the dessert.

Nutrition Info (Per Serving): Kcal 287, Fat 18g, Net Carbs 6.1g, Protein 4.4g

Lemon Mug Cake

Preparation Time: 5 minutes

Cooking Time: 2 minutes

Servings: 1

Ingredients:

- 1 egg, lightly beaten
- 1/2 tsp. lemon rind
- 1 tbsp. butter, melted
- 1 1/2 tbsp. fresh lemon juice
- 2 tbsp. erythritol
- 1/4 tsp. baking powder, gluten-free
- 1/4 cup almond flour

Directions:

1. In a bowl or container, mix almond flour, baking powder, and sweetener.
2. Add egg, lemon juice, and melted butter in almond flour mixture and whisk until well combined.
3. Pour cake mixture into the microwave-safe mug and microwave for 90 seconds.
4. Serve and enjoy.

Nutrition:

Calories: 275 Fats: 5.9g Fiber: 2.4g Carbohydrates: 1.3 g Protein: 4.1g

Strawberry Mousse

Preparation Time: 10 minutes

Cooking Time: 5 minutes

Servings: 2

Ingredients:

- 1 cup heavy whipping cream
- 1 cup fresh strawberries, chopped
- 2 tbsp. Swerve
- 1 cup cream cheese

Directions:

1. Add heavy whipping cream in a bowl and beat until thickened using a hand mixer.
2. Add sweetener and cream cheese and beat well. Add strawberries and fold well.
3. Pour in serving glasses and place in the refrigerator for 1-2 hours. Serve chilled and enjoy.

Nutrition:

Calories: 219 Fat: 8g Fiber: 3.1g Carbohydrates: 1.9 g Protein: 1.2g

www.ingramcontent.com/pod-product-compliance
Lightning Source LLC
Chambersburg PA
CBHW062343300326
41947CB00012B/1189